Polish Heavy Military Motorcycle P.Z.Inż. M111 „Sokół 1000"

Basic Version

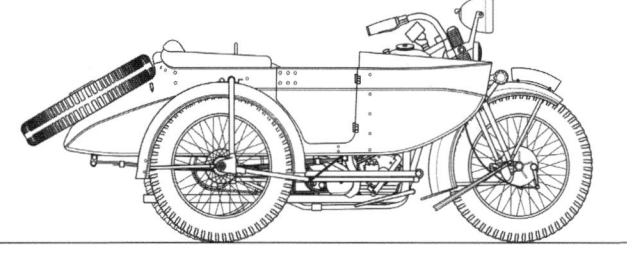

1/35

1/17.5

Drawings: Adam Jońca

Armed Version
ckm 7.9 mm wz. 30.

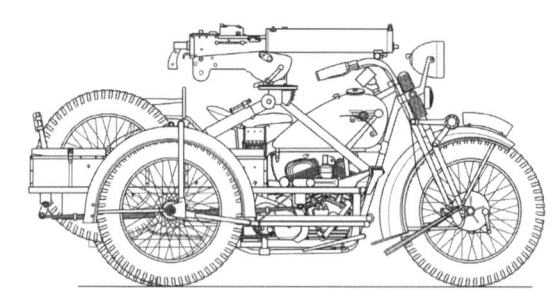

1/35

1/17.5

Communication version.
RKD radio station
ROD receiver.

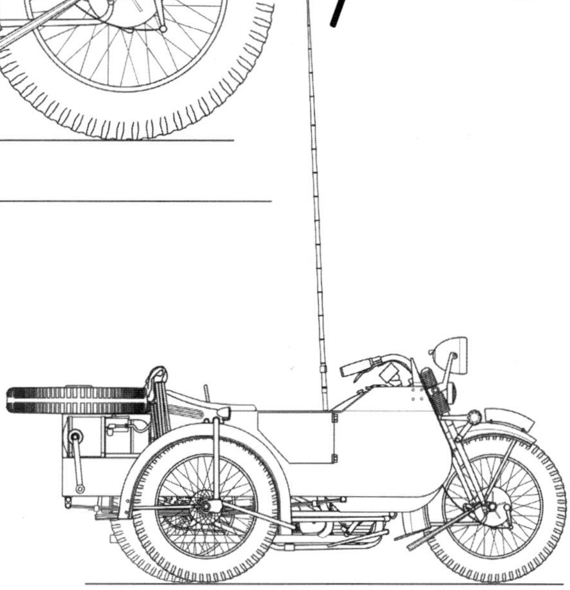

1/35

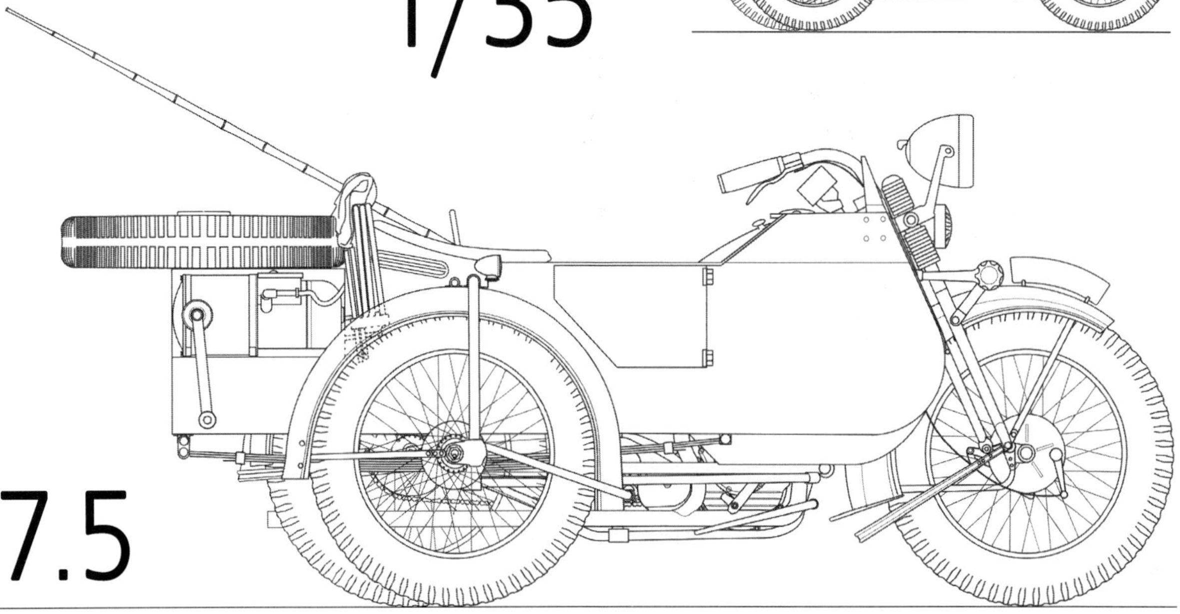

1/17.5

Drawings: Adam Jońca

Origins

CWS M55 – one of the prototypes with an individual C.W.S. PR.5 number plate.

CWS M55 of the S-III series at the Armoured Weapons Training Centre in Modlin Fortress.

Military CWS 55 lent to a motorbike club for the rally.

Nr.1 i 2/XIII

Typ aktualny
w produkcji bież.

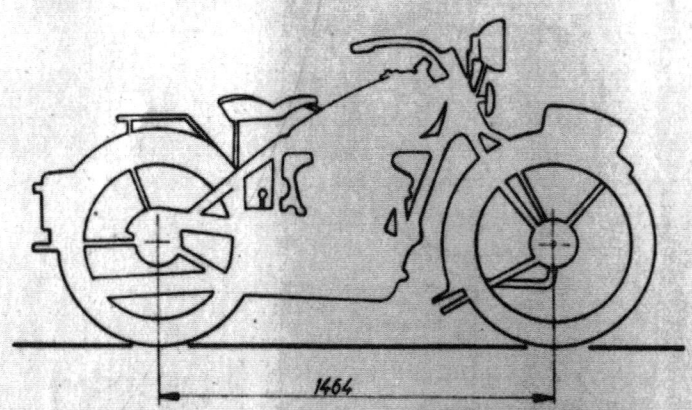

1464

Motocykl typ S-1000 wykonywany w 2-ch wariantach

a/ Podwozie typ S-1000 /z przyczepką/   -

   Silnik Nr.XIII typ S-1000   - moc 22 KM

   Nośność użyteczna podwozia   - 3 ludzi

   Ciężar własny motocykla z przyczepką   - 375 kg.

   Szybkość maksymalna   - 100 km/godz.

b/ Podwozie typ S-1000 /z przyczepką i napędem
                  na koło wózka/   -

   Silnik Nr.XIII typ S-1000   - moc 22 MK

   Nośność użyteczna podwosia   - 3 ludzi

   Ciężar własny motocykla   - 395 kg.

   Szybkość maksymalna w terenie   - 60 km/godz.

Produkowany seryjnie. Model z napędem na koło przyczepki w opraco-
waniu rysunkowym.

B.S. 259 E. 22.11.37. 2000.   Szymański i Cygański W-wa, Wilcza 32.

One of the pages from the 1937 Armoured Weapons Equipment Album. This was a catalogue published as a collection of light copies in perhaps several dozen copies (first edition - October 1936, later updated).

Pictured above are M111 motorcycles at the factory. They were produced in 1934.

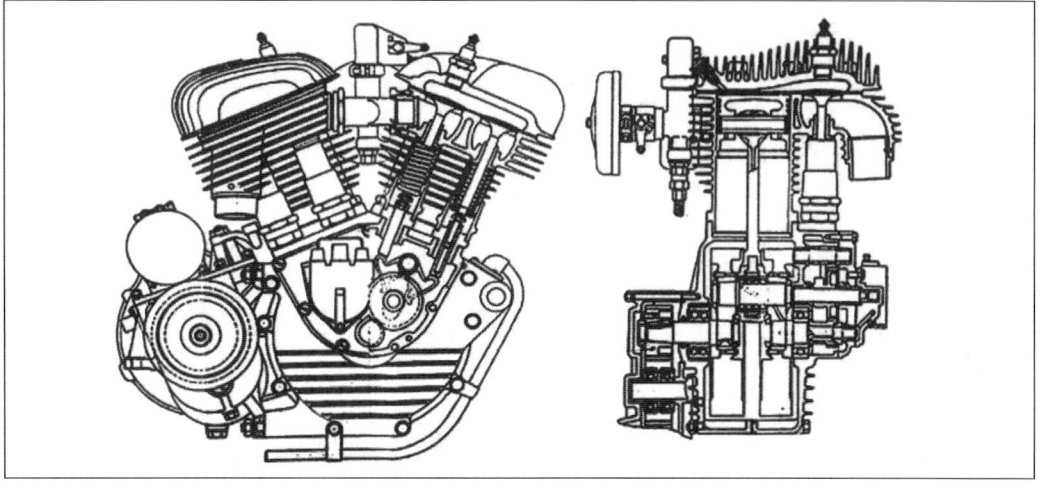

M 111 motorbike engine – drawing taken from the service manual (several editions).

The engine of the M 111 motorbike from the left.

The engine of the M 111 motorbike in view on the right.

6

The M 111 motorbike pictured here dates from 1935. It has the military registration number 1420 and served in the 5th Armoured Battalion (Krakow).

Bottom left – M 111 in front view. In the right photos, front and rear suspension of the motorcycle.

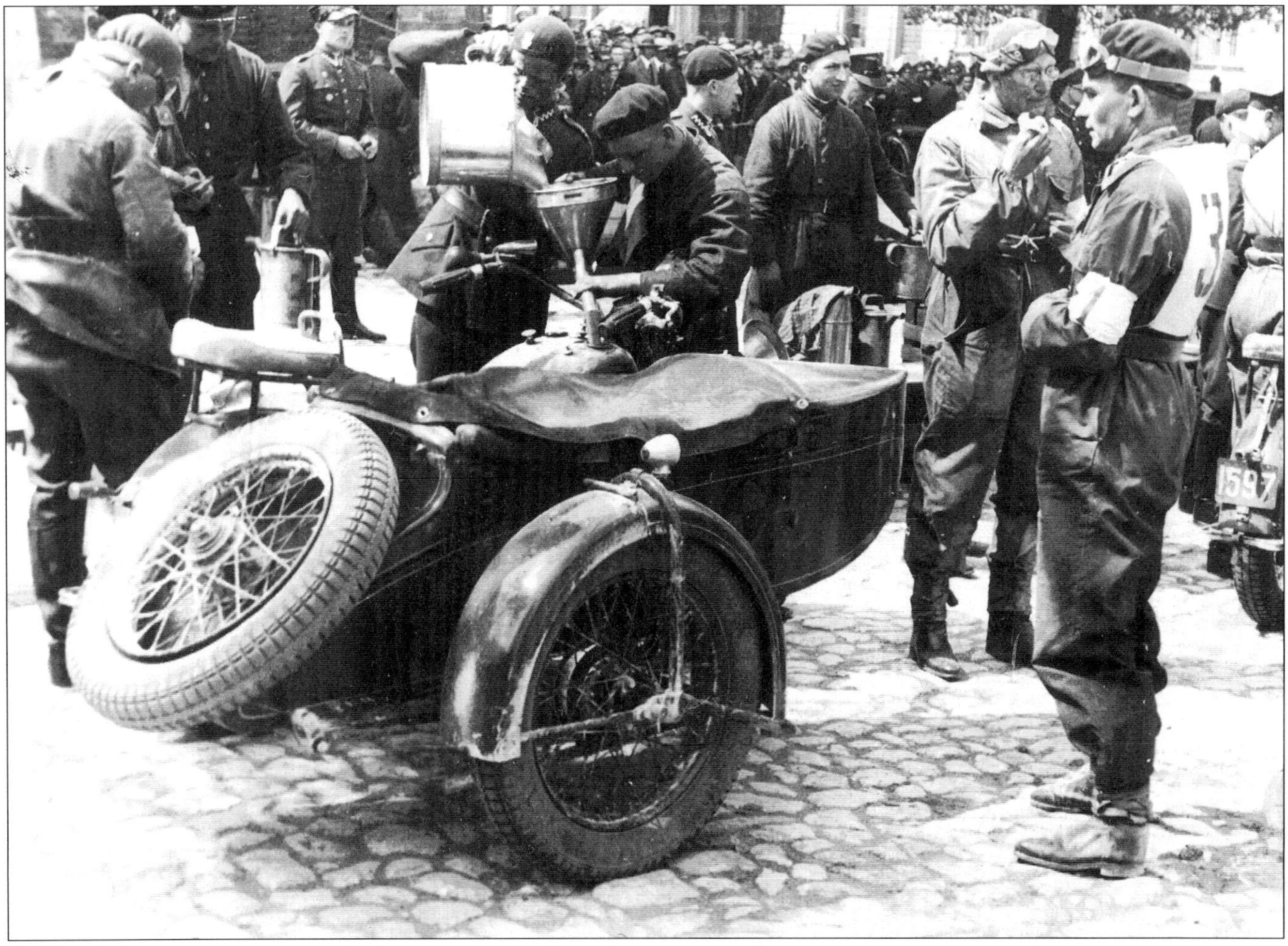
1597

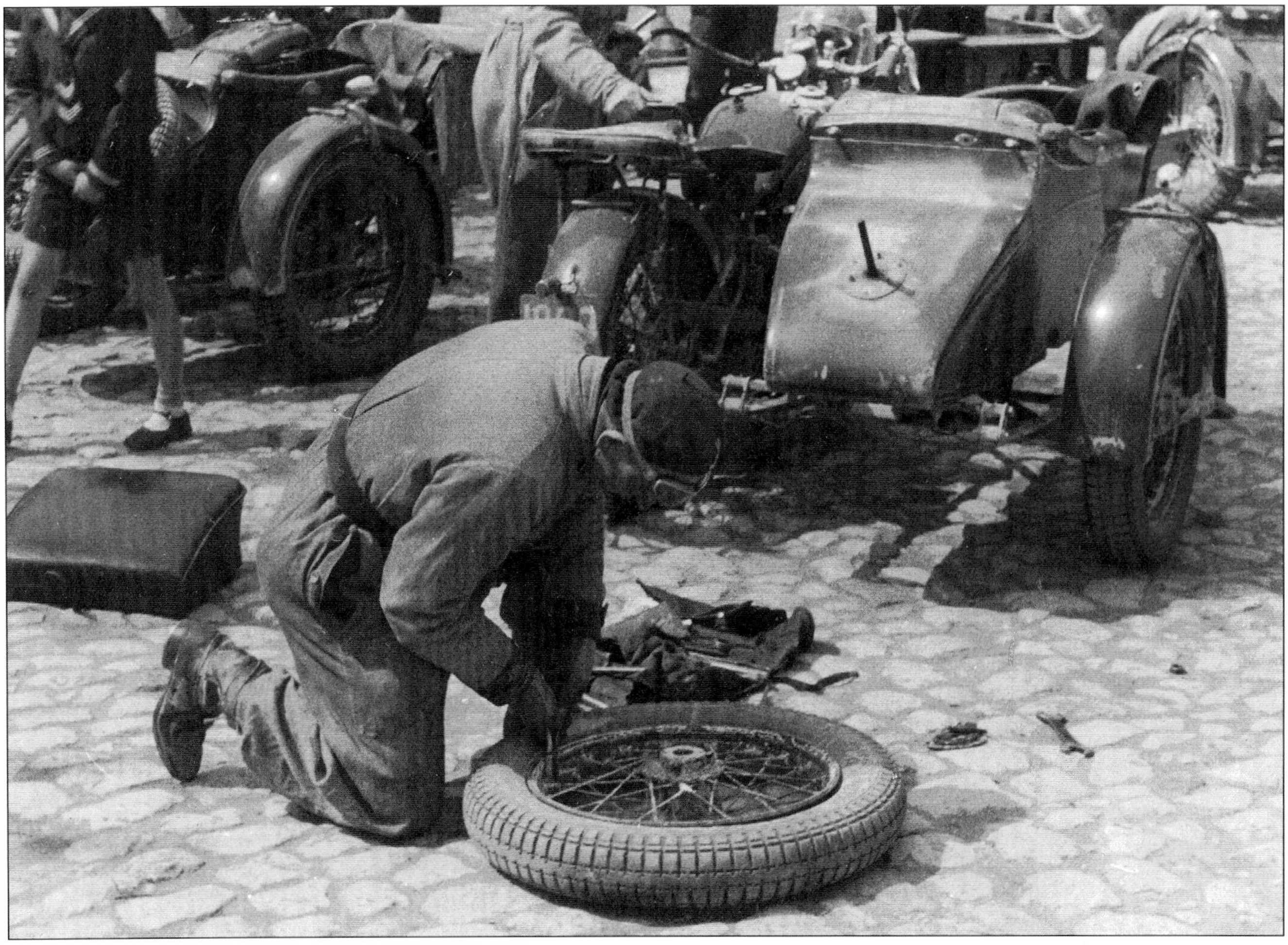

On the page opposite, the bogie of the M 111 motorbike. Photos from a rally in 1937.

The motorcycle was exactly what the army wanted. It wasn't 'modern' because it wasn't meant to be. It was not designed to break down; more importantly, it was designed to be difficult to break down. Everything on it was designed with plenty of room - so it was undoubtedly too heavy. But it had enough power and durability to take on terrain that no Harley-Davidson, even one with a 1200 hp engine, could match. It also had the advantage of being simple to build - maintenance and much of the repair work could be done in the field.

In the service

Motorcyclists of the Drivers' School of the 2nd Tank Battalion departing from Żurawica near Przemyśl. Photo from 1934.

M111 motorbike of the 1st Horse Rifle Regiment stationed at Garwolin (motorised regiment in 1939). Motorbike with plate "Learn to Drive".

Motorbike M 111 in front of the former Prussian vehicle depot in Poznań, used between the wars as garages for the 1st Tank Regiment, 1st Armoured Regiment, 1st Tank and Armoured Car Battalion and finally 1st Armoured Battalion.

Top of the page: – on the left is an M 111 motorbike in the 4th Armoured Battalion from Brest (year 1936), and on the right a motorbike from the cadre 9th Armoured Battalion.

Reconnaissance patrol motorcycle. A soldier of the 10th Horse Rifle Regiment poses for a photograph. The regiment was motorised and incorporated into the 10th Cavalry Brigade.

Photo taken during an exercise of the motorised 24th Lancers Regiment (part of the 10th Cavalry Brigade).

At the head of an armoured car platoon wz.34 motorbike of the platoon commander – 8ᵗʰ Armoured Battalion, Bydgoszcz, 11 June 1936 (Battalion Day).

One of the few photos of M 111 in camouflage painting – motorbike with military registration number 1847 from 26ᵗʰ Companion Squadron (Lublin R-XIII aircraft are also visible).

M 111 in the field. The motorcycle is numbered 1585 and belongs to the 8th Armoured Battalion from Bydgoszcz. The photo was taken on 11 June 1936.

Motorbike 1095 on parade in Poznań. It was not possible to determine what its affiliation - it is possible that we see the forehead 7th EOD Battalion.

Motorbikes in aviation. Registration numbers 1503 and 1499 – 4th Aviation Regiment, Toruń.

Display of Polish military equipment in Romania. Bukareszt, 1934. In the foreground motorcycle no. 1383, next to a TKS tank, in the background a Polish FIAT 621L truck.

Armed motorbikes. Ckm 7.9 mm wz.30 Browning.

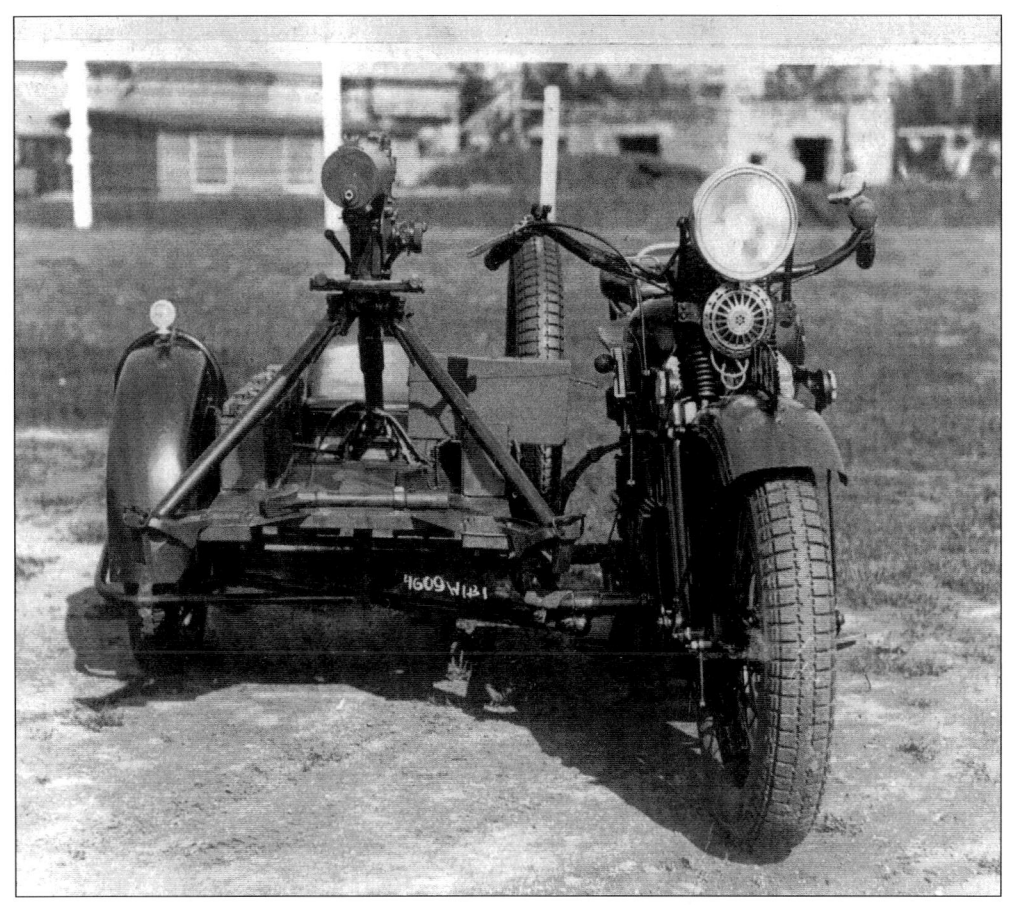

Below and on the next page is motorcycle 1433 with ckm wz.30. These are photos from 1935, already after the changes. It was sent to the 3rd Rifle Battalion as a specimen.

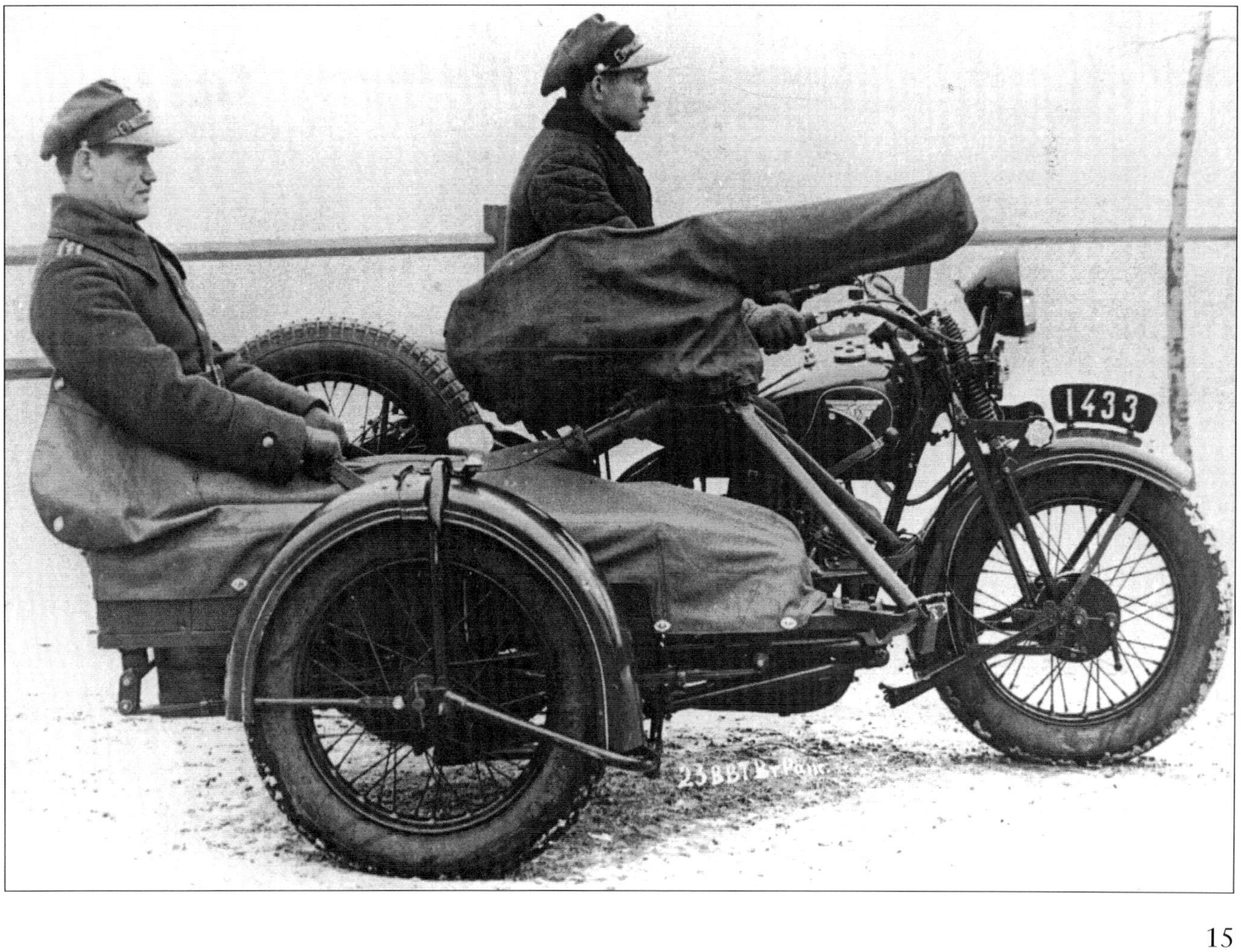

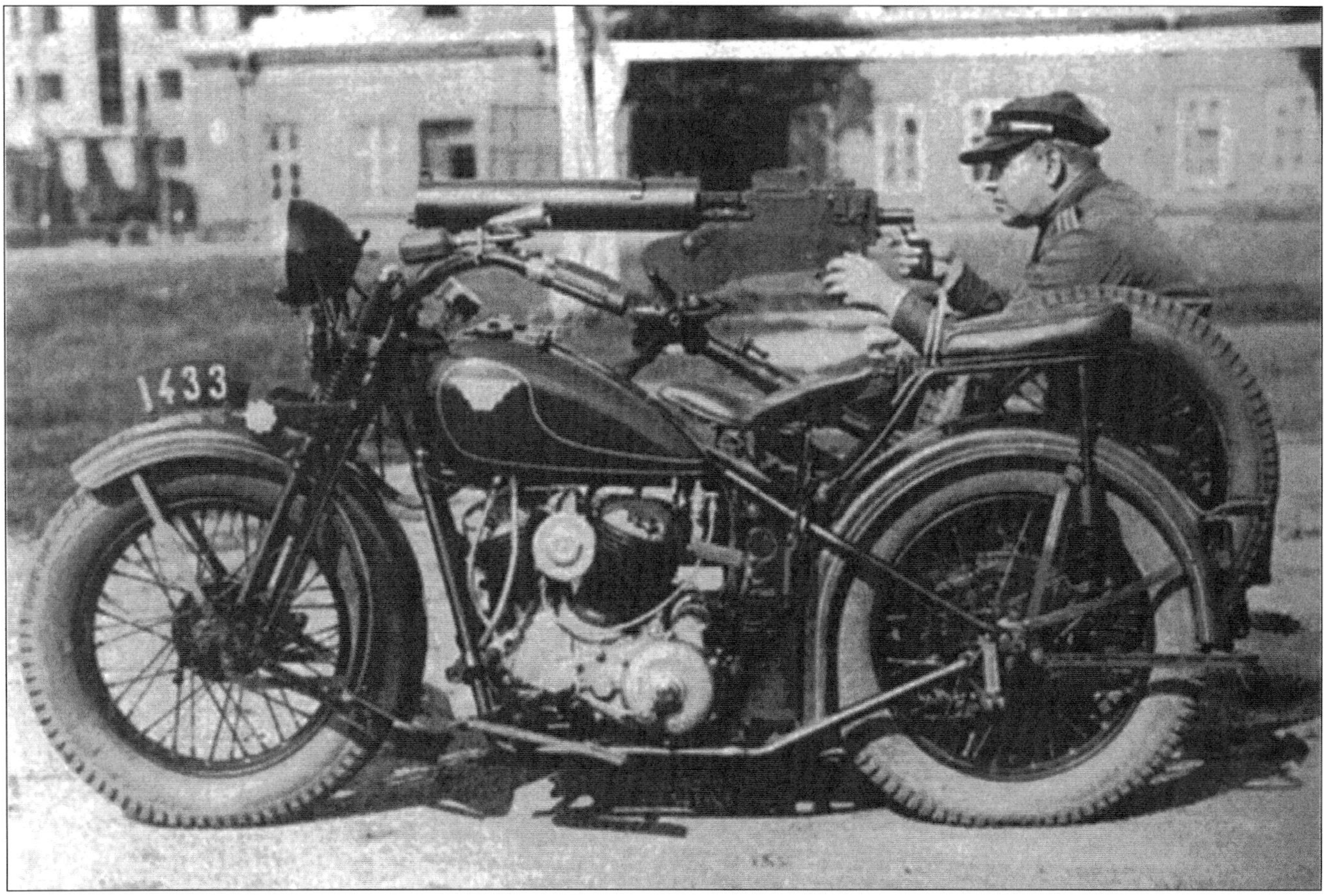

Model specimen of M 111 no. 1433 with ckm wz.30. 3rd Rifle Battalion, 1935.

Demonstration of motorcycle number 2099 in 1938 at the Cavalry Training Centre in Grudziądz. Ckm wz.30 set up for anti-aircraft shooting.

Motrocycle no. 1883 in a photograph taken on 3 May 1938 in Warsaw's Mokotow Field.

Ckm wz.30 during anti-aircraft shooting.

Armed motorbikes. Rkm 7.9 mm wz.28 Browning.

Motorcycle with plate number 2304, armed with rkm. The weapon mount is unusually embedded without drilling through the plating. A soldier of the 10th Horse Rifle Regiment poses for a photograph.

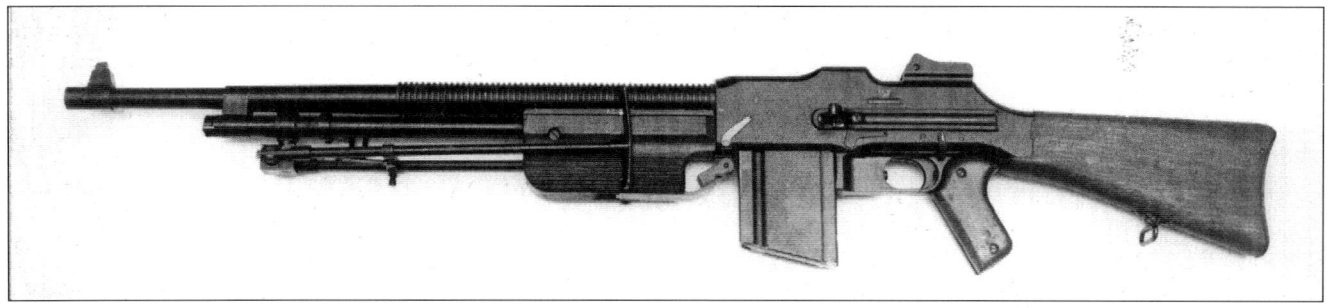

Hand-held machine gun wz.28.

Technical drawing of the machine gun handle as recommended in 1936.

Technical drawing of the trolley with machine gun handle. The carabiner cover was not used in practice.

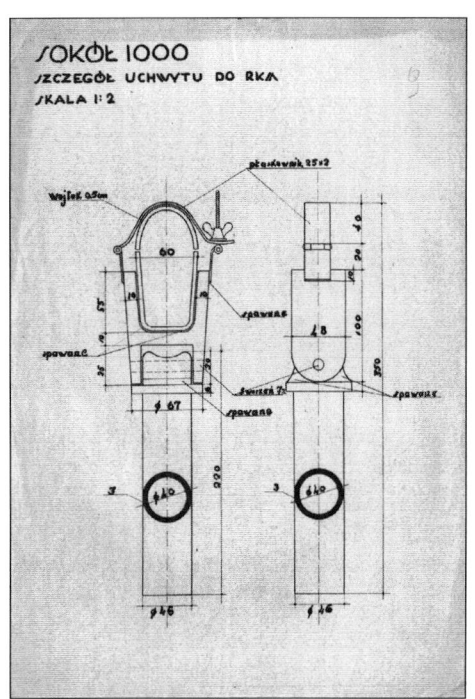

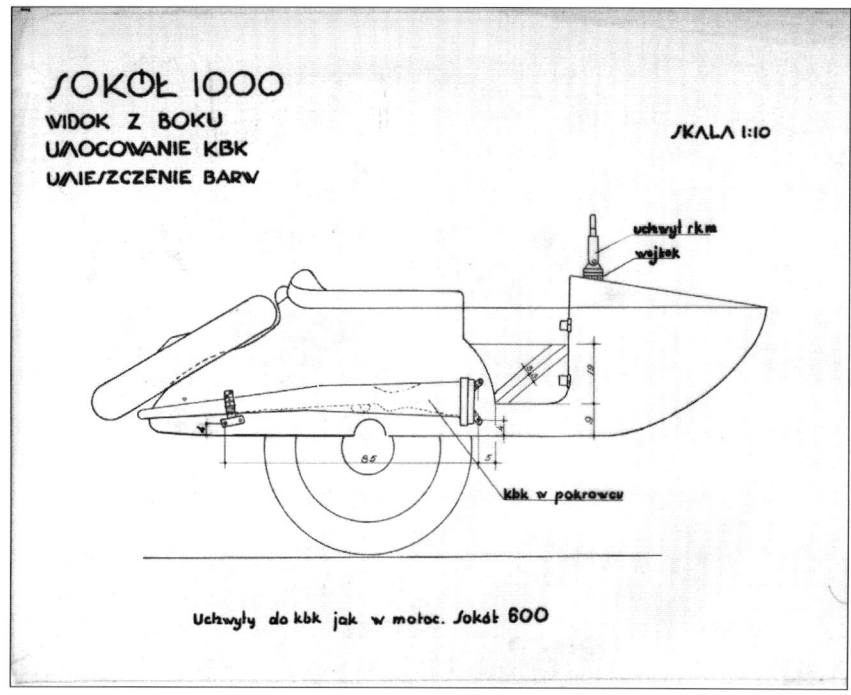

Armed motorbikes.
Antitank mines.

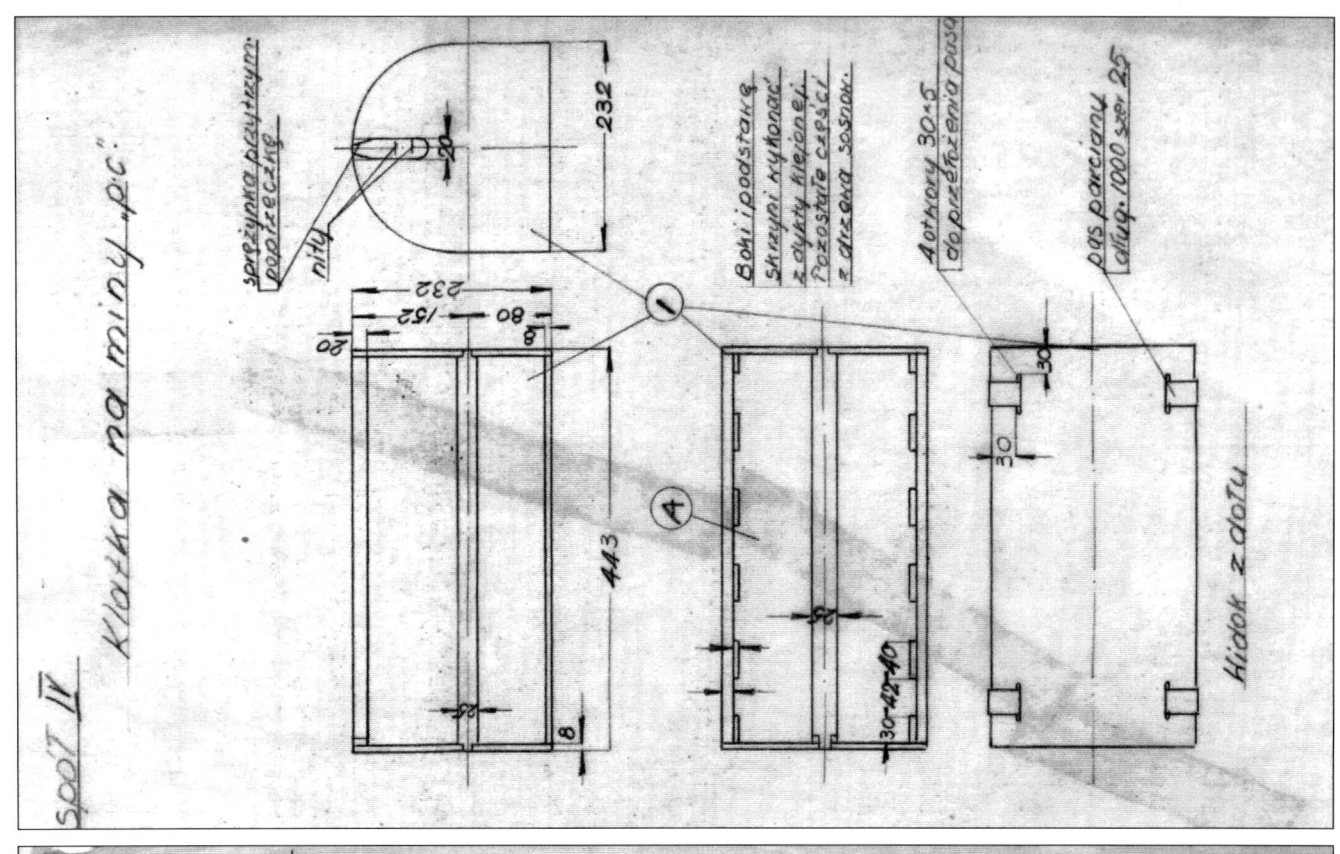

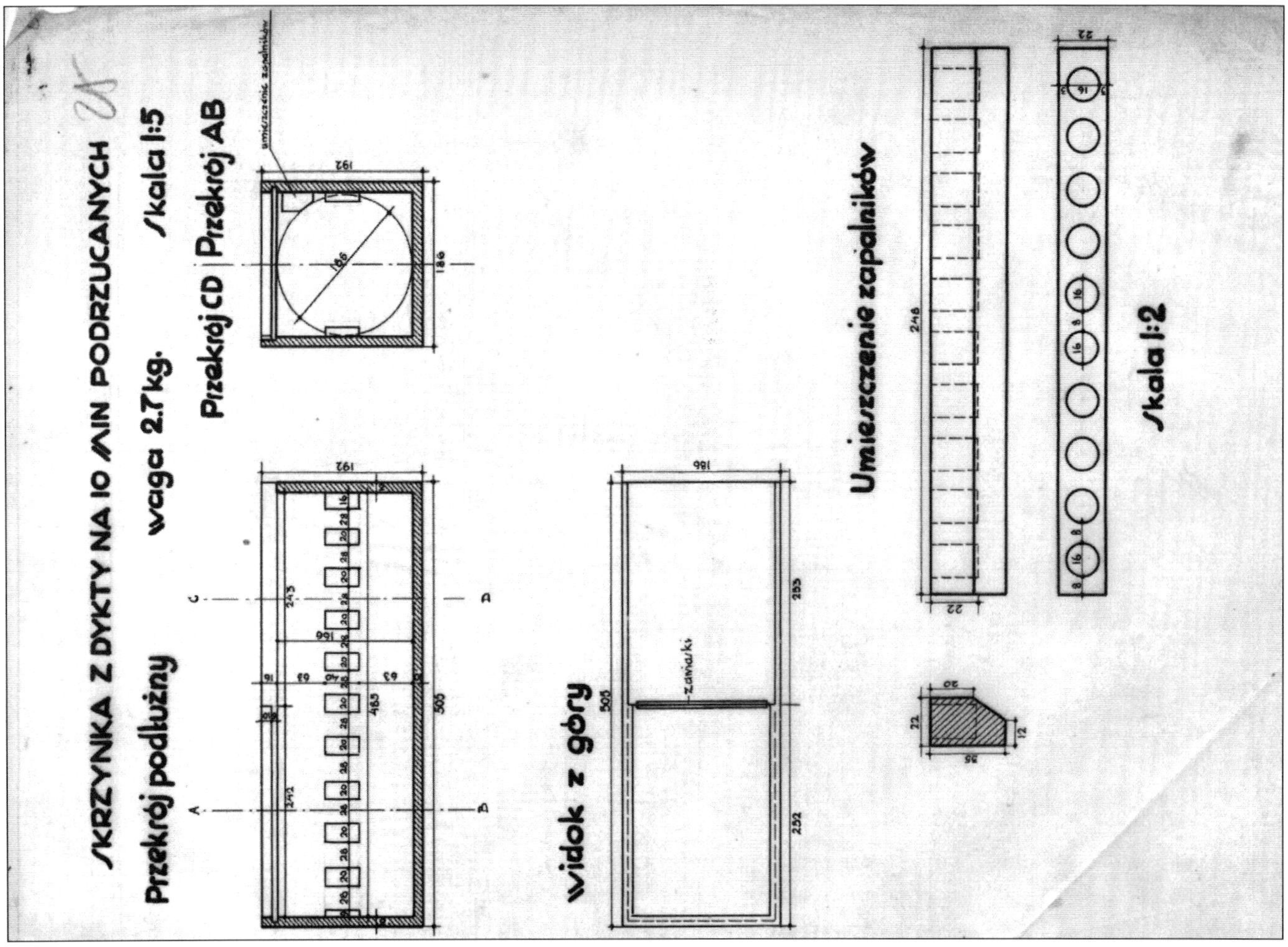

Barrier platoon on the march..

Motorbike with military registration number 2309 of the barrier platoon. A wooden box for 10 anti-tank mine bodies leaning against the boogie.

Motorbike
with radio

Motorcycle 1075 with tarpaulin up. Between the motorbike and the boogie are the tubes of a folding mast for stationary work (with a longer reach), to the right of the boogie is a bamboo mast for marching work.

Motorcycle trolley 1075 with bamboo mast and telescopic mast mounted. RKD radio transmitter in a canvas cover strapped to the front of the trolley, ROD receiver inside the trolley on the right. At the rear of the trolley are the spare wheel, alternator and prop box.

Demonstrations in Warsaw – on the sides of a radio-controlled Polish FIAT 508 ride motorbikes 1286 and 1075 with RKD radio stations.

Motorbike 1075 with RKD radio. The transmitter, in its case, positioned. At the front of the cart. On the left the receiver ROD of a newer design.

Below are photos of motorcycle number 1286. Converted car - transmitter on the front of the car, under the top cover, on top of the ROD receiver in the cover, and on top a document bag. The two masts erected - a bamboo mast for working while travelling, and a high foldable mast for stationary work, allowing communication over longer distances.

Motorcycle number 1286 with ROD radio station at the 1934 Romanian display.

Mokotowskie. The front of the vehicle was fitted with a new type of ROD, wz.33. In the handles on the left side of the boogie, a bamboo antenna mast.

RKD radio transmitter – It was housed in a wooden box measuring 47x31x21.5 cm.

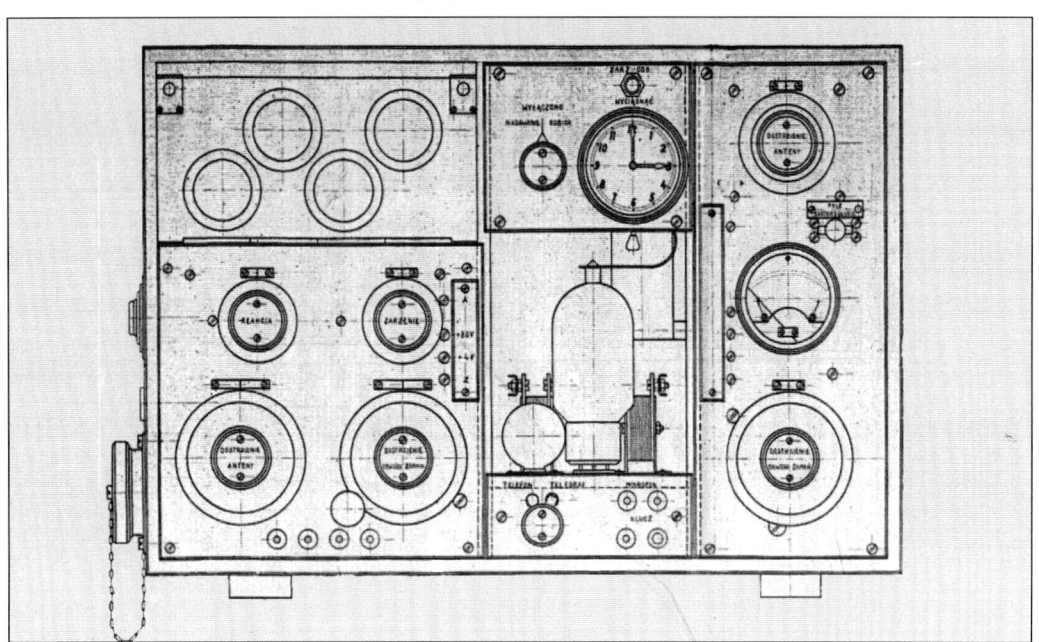

Technical drawing of the RKD transmitter.

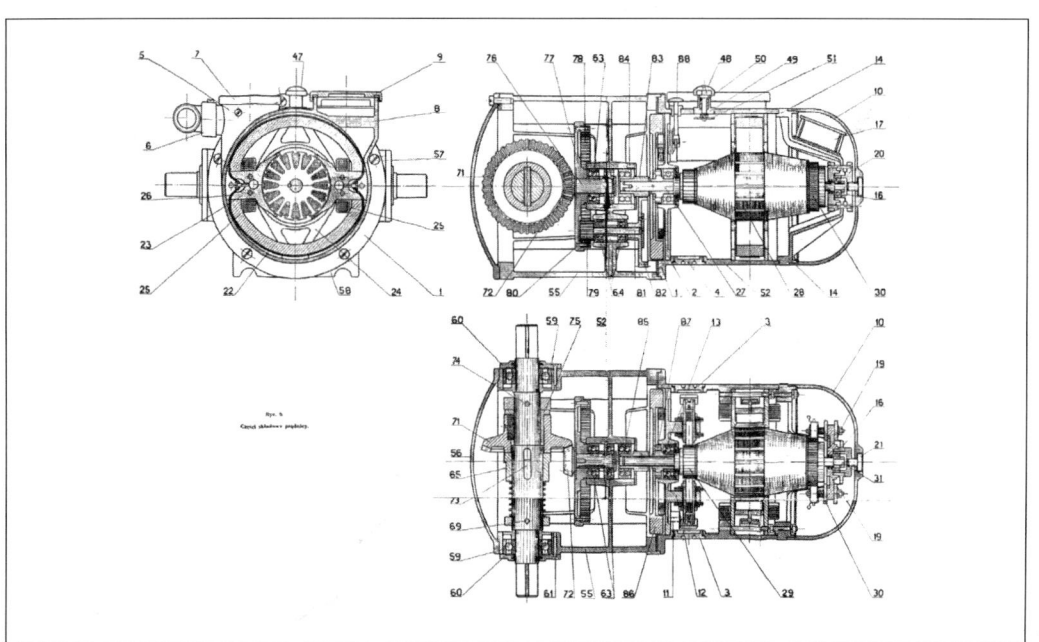

Technical drawing of the handheld alternator of the RKD radio station. The battery box had dimensions of 41x30x17 cm and was placed on the bottom of the boogie.

Powered motorbike trolley

The idea to improve the off-road capability of the moto-cycles was to also drive the sidecar wheel. The drive of the bogie wheel was solved in such a way that it was transferred from the rear wheel via two gears to a shaft with a flexible joint, and from the shaft again to two gears and the bogie wheel. The prototype was ready in the summer of 1938. The army was eventually interested in this design, but it remained in the P.Z.Inż. product range until September 1939.

Production and development programme

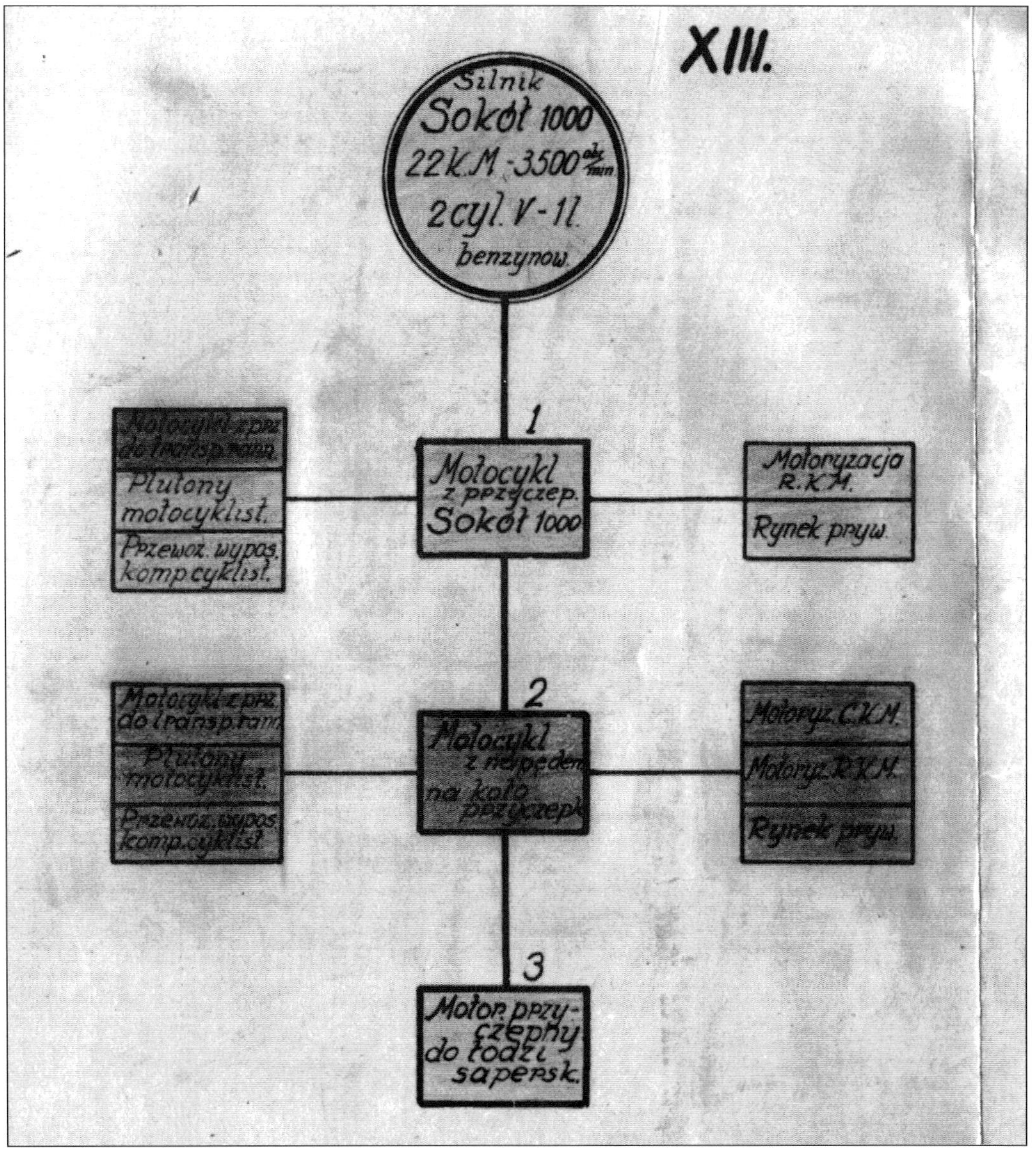

As late as 1937, the State Engineering Works planned to maintain the production of M111 motorbikes (with the new name "Sokół 1000"). The programme envisaged the production of 1000 ccm motorbikes with a bogie in segment 1 for motorcyclists' pluton, with a cap for transporting the wounded, carrying equipment in cyclists' companies, motorising rkm's and for the private market. Segment 2, would include motorbikes with bogie wheel drive and in addition to applications as in segment 1. also to motorise ckm. The 3rd segment is the production of engines – including outboard engines for sapper boats.

Motorcyclist's uniform

Left photo: 1934, an exhibition of Polish motorcycle equipment in Romania. Motorcycle M111 with registration number 1359. The motorcyclist is wearing a mantle, i.e. a variant of the protective suit worn over the uniform. The driver wears a leather hauberk (so-called leather helmet) of non-Moscow design from the First World War - such haubuks were produced in Poland, but we do not know how many there were (at least several dozen). Both 'passengers' are wearing steel, French-designed tank helmets. On the photo to the right, on the motorcycle 1859, a motorcyclist of the 2nd Armoured Battalion (Żurawica). Leather jacket No. 19 (with armoured weapon inserts sewn on the collar), leather cap with earflaps "pilotka", leather gloves "musketeers", high boots "saperki".

Motorcyclists of the 8th Armoured Battalion in the June 1936 photo - privates and sergeants in leather jackets wz.19, the officer on the left, with a sword, wears the newly introduced leather half coat wz.36. French pattern tank helmets, high boots.

The motorbike (W04-03) is manned by men wearing combat uniforms, which began to be introduced in 1939.

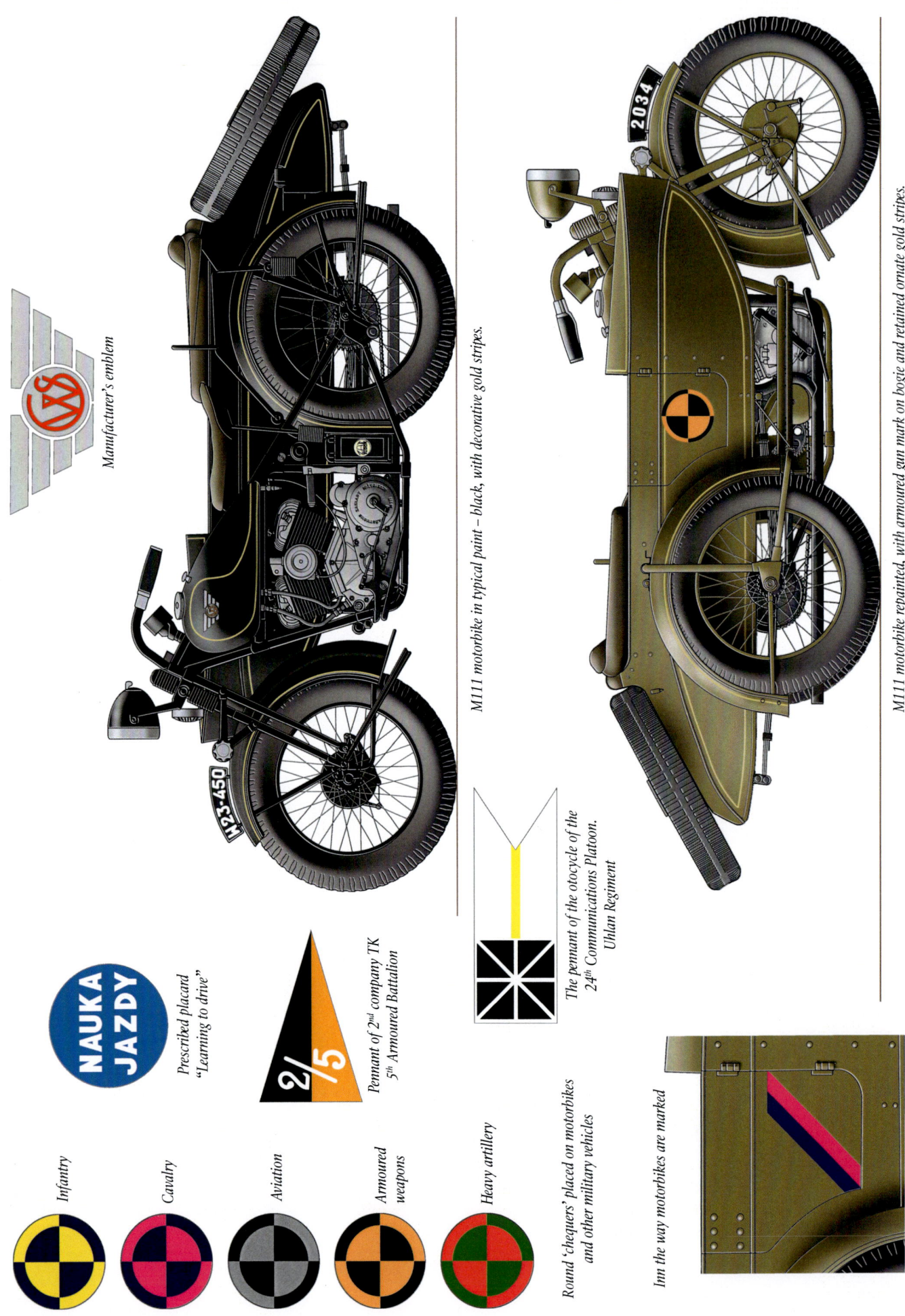

Manufacturer's emblem

M111 motorbike in typical paint – black, with decorative gold stripes.

M111 motorbike repainted, with armoured gun mark on bogie and retained ornate gold stripes.

NAUKA JAZDY

Prescribed placard "Learning to drive"

2/5

Pennant of 2nd company TK 5th Armoured Battalion

The pennant of the otocycle of the 24th Communications Platoon. Uhlan Regiment

Infantry

Cavalry

Aviation

Armoured weapons

Heavy artillery

Round 'chequers' placed on motorbikes and other military vehicles

Inn the way motorbikes are marked

28